I0817364

¡Nuestra maravillosa Tierra!
Our Exciting Earth!

OCÉANOS
OCEANS

Claire Romaine
traducido por / translated by Eida de la Vega

Please visit our website, www.garethstevens.com. For a free color catalog of all our high-quality books, call toll free 1-800-542-2595 or fax 1-877-542-2596.

Cataloging-in-Publication Data

Names: Romaine, Claire.
Title: Oceans = Océanos / Claire Romaine.
Description: New York : Gareth Stevens Publishing, 2018. | Series: Our exciting Earth! = ¡Nuestra maravillosa Tierra! | In English and Spanish | Includes index.
Identifiers: ISBN 9781538215340 (library bound)
Subjects: LCSH: Ocean–Juvenile literature. | Oceanography–Juvenile literature.
Classification: LCC GC21.5 R65 2018 | DDC 551.46–dc23

Published in 2018 by
Gareth Stevens Publishing
111 East 14th Street, Suite 349
New York, NY 10003

Copyright © 2018 Gareth Stevens Publishing

Translator: Eida de la Vega
Editorial Director, Spanish: Nathalie Beullens-Maoui
Editor: Therese Shea
Designer: Bethany Perl

Photo credits: Cover, p. 1 Galyna Andrushko/Shutterstock.com; p. 5 Veronika Vankova/Shutterstock.com; p. 7 Melanie Hobson/Shutterstock.com; p. 9 Tischenko Irina/Shutterstock.com; p. 11 Franco Banfi/WaterFrame/ Getty Images; pp. 13, 24 SARWUT KUNDEJ/Shutterstock.com; pp. 15, 24 stephan kerkhofs/Shuttestock.com; pp. 17, 24 Laura Dinraths/Shutterstock.com; p. 19 Jurjen Veerman/Shutterstock.com; pp. 21, 24 Aleksey Stemmer/Shutterstock.com; p. 23 Alexey Y. Petrov/Shutterstock.com.

All rights reserved. No part of this book may be reproduced in any form without permission in writing from the publisher, except by a reviewer.

Printed in the United States of America

CPSIA compliance information: Batch #CW18GS: For further information contact Gareth Stevens, New York, New York at 1-800-542-2595.

Contenido

Contents

¡Vamos al océano!

•••••••••••••••••••••••••••••

Let's go to the ocean!

Los océanos son grandes.
Contienen agua salada.

Oceans are big.
They contain salt water.

En el océano hay muchos animales. ¡Los peces son solo una clase de ellos!

....

The ocean has many animals. Fish are just one kind!

¡El animal más grande
del océano es
la ballena azul!

....

The biggest
ocean animal is
the blue whale!

Los corales son
animales del océano.
¡Parecen plantas!

....

Corals are
ocean animals.
They look like plants!

Los animales del océano necesitan las plantas del océano. ¡Las tortugas marinas se las comen!

....

Ocean animals need ocean plants.
Sea turtles eat them!

El pasto marino es una
planta del océano.
¡Los caballitos de mar
se esconden ahí!

....

Sea grass is an
ocean plant.
Sea horses hide in it!

El agua del océano sube y baja. Esa es una marea. ¡La luna y el sol causan las mareas!

....

Ocean water rises and falls. This is a tide. The moon and sun cause tides!

Buscamos animales
del océano.
¡Veo un cangrejo!

....

We look for
ocean animals.
I see a crab!

Nadamos en el océano. ¡Los océanos son divertidos!

....

We swim in the ocean. Oceans are fun!

Palabras que debes aprender
Words to Know

(los) corales
corals

(el) cangrejo
crab

(el) caballito de mar
sea horse

(la) tortuga marina
sea turtle

Índice / Index